Quitterie and Daniel Cazes

D0521425

DISCOVERING TOULOUSE

Photographs by Bertrand Cabrol

Translation by Juan-Paolo Perré

SUD OUEST

Toulouse has always been the gateway to the Midi : regularly swept by the South winds, the city offers visitors access to a Mediterranean world thanks to its geographical location, its climate and its culture. Today, the personality of this large metropolis, often divided between tradition and modernity, is the result of its history and the men who shaped it. Beyond the vision of a "pink city" which emerges from a superficial regard, Toulouse was receptive to the arts, "holy" for its dozens of churches, and commercial and agricultural because it always knew how to profit from its situation and its environment. The city's building materials take the visitor back to Antiquity : brick has been the dominant building material in Toulouse for more than twenty centuries. The prices of stone which had to be transported by boat were well-known : marble from the Pyrenees and limestone brought by way of the Garonne River, overshadowed since the 17th century by marble from Caunes-Minervois in the Aude region and stone brought from Carcassonne by way of the Canal du Midi. Little remains of the glorious Antiquity of Toulouse. Here and there, vestiges of the rampart which surrounded the city at the beginning of the first century A.D. can bee seen. This enclosure, useful only for prestige in these times of peace, once symbolized the city's might. Toulouse owed its fortune to the fact that it was a meeting point for trade between the Mediterranean Sea and the Atlantic, more than any other port on the Garonne, onto which the

city freely opened. It was only in the third century that the insecurity of the times prompted the construction of a new rampart along the river (visible at the Institut Catholique). The Roman monuments have disappeared : if the remains of one of the largest theaters in the Roman world have been found near the Pont Neuf, if the aqueduct still appeared on maps of the city in the 17th century, the temples and the forum exist only in our memory. Antiquity survives nonetheless in the orthogonal layout of the city's central streets, parting from the principal north-south artery, which is now a pedestrian zone (Rue Saint-Rome, Rue des Changes, Rue des Filatiers). The end of Antiquity brought the churches : in the center, the cathedral and the Daurade, outside of the walls the funereal basilicas, the most noteworthy of which is Saint-Sernin. We know little of the "congested capital" (described by Mr. Roquebert) of the Visigoth kingdom (between 418 and 507), the famous Reino de Tolosa that the Spanish consider as the foundation of their own monarchy. The following centuries remain quite obscure. Urban development began again after the year 1000. The city's expansion towards the North, begun in the 11th century, is demarcated by another rampart. Saint-Sernin was the center of the new Bourg, accompanied by Saint-Pierre-des-Cuisines on the bank of the Garonne. Another district, Saint-Cyprien, sprang up on the opposite bank and was also surrounded by a rampart in the 14th century.

From the end of the 11th century to the 14th century, religious architecture saw a period of effervescence and renewal ; the same was certainly true for secular architecture, about which less is known. Toulouse came under the dominion of the king of France in 1271, after three centuries during which had seen the city at its apogee, dominating the Midi as far East as the Rhône. After the disastrous period of the wars, the famines and the plagues of the 14th century, the city recovered its vitality with the revival of trade and experienced a true golden age beginning in the middle of the 15th century with the growth in pastel farming. Dazzling fortunes were built and resulted in the creation of mansions which were often veritable palaces. Wealth opened the doors of the noblesse de robe to certain members of the bourgeoisie, whether by carefully arranged marriages or by accession to the ennobling post of magistrate (announced at the time by the construction of a tower). The collapse in the pastel trade and the wars of religion caused a new era of difficulties. However, thanks to the traditional farming of wheat, which could be marketed by way of the Canal du Midi - that extraordinary economic tool - the bourgeois were able to safely establish their fortunes. The city was then able to install facilities which, apart from pleasure and prestige, also served the needs of trade (promenades around the Grand-Rond, construction of the Hôtel de Ville and the Place du Capitole, renovation of the wharves...). In the 19th century,

At the center of the Place Wilson, the garden with the statue of the native Languedoc poet Godolin (1580-1649).

The façade of the Capitole. (Photo Jean-Paul Gisserot)

The pediment of the Capitole. (Photo Jean-Paul Gisserot)

these revenues were no longer sufficient, and industry failed to develop. Caught up in the fever of grand city planning inspired by Baron Haussman, Toulouse installed two large avenues - Rue d'Alsace-Lorraine and Rue de Metz - whose buildings clearly demonstrate the break which they represent with traditional values.

Now in full expansion, invigorated by prestigious industries, Toulouse is searching for its identity and sometimes finding it. Endowed with an image of vitality, the city continues to expand its facilities, rediscovers its brick facades, but still hesitates. Pastiche dominates local architecture, the city's culture only timidly dares to embrace the contemporary and sometimes rejects its own past riches, and the shadow of Barcelona causes

concern. But the vibrant charm of its narrow streets, the moving beauty of certain spots, the pleasure of losing oneself in other times and of finding oneself all of a sudden on the terrace of a cafe, invite the visitor to stroll, to become a resident of the city ; this is the discovery to which we invite you.

THE PLACE WILSON

Since its creation in the 19th century under the name of the Place Villeneuve, the Place Wilson is the monumental entrance to the heart of Toulouse. The plan to renovate this space, formed by the meeting of the antique rampart of the City and the medieval rampart of the Bourg, took form between 1805 and 1834. A large avenue leading from the Canal du Midi to the oval square opened a large

breach in the belt formed by the boulevards. Today, these radiating streets provide access to several neighborhoods of the city. The fountain, the statue of Godolin and the vegetation represent the mildness of life and temper the rigid order of the buildings, far-removed heirs of the *insulae* of Rome and Ostia.

THE CAPITOLE

The term Capitole evokes more an antique temple than a city hall, and yet... There was indeed a Capitole in Toulouse - a sanctuary dedicated to Jupiter, Juno and Minerva - of which we know only (by way of the "Passion de Saint Saturnin") that it had a large stairway ; its location remains unknown. The name given to the city hall results from the resemblance

On the following pages :
The Capitole's Salle des Illustres ; created between 1892 and 1898 by Paul Pujol, it is decorated with paintings and sculptures by J.-P. Laurens, B. Constant, Rixens, and others.

between the Latin words *capitulum* (municipal chapter) and *capitolium* (Capitole). The similarity was used to associate the assembly of municipal magistrates with the ancient Roman Senate. Originally (at the beginning of the 12th century), the "consuls", representatives of the new merchant class, arbitrated affairs between merchants along with judges named by the county. At the end of the 12th century, they possessed numerous regulatory, judicial, financial and military powers. After 1271, the kings of France confirmed their privileges, but their powers were gradually taken over, first by the seneschal, then by the Parliament beginning in 1443, and finally

8

Detail from "Les Bords de la Garonne", by Henri Martin, who, with his panels representing the Seasons, created the best paintings preserved in the Capitole.

by the Intendant of Languedoc beginning in the 17th century.

The acquisition of buildings by the consuls in 1190 represented their desire to establish themselves as a distinct power, at the opposite end of the City from the residence of the count. The magistrates, who remained in office for a term of only a year, never succeeded in constructing a coherent monumental group of buildings.

In the small district which gradually took form on the current site of the Capitole and the Square de Gaulle, a number of large buildings were constructed in the Middle Ages and coldly demolished in the 19th century. The one remaining is the "Donjon", the former Tour des Archives completed in 1530 ; its slate roof was redone in 1873 by Viollet-le-Duc, who also added a belfry. Currently a passage between the two squares, the Cour Henri

IV was built at the very beginning of the 17th century according to the plans of the architect Souffron ; the portal, built by Bachelier in 1546, is topped by a statue of the king. The current facade, designed by Guillaume Cammas, was intended to conceal the heterogeneous buildings of the old Maison Commune. Construction began in 1750, when the square did not yet exist (it would not be finished until a century later). From the classical rhythm of Cammas' elevation emerges the central portico ; the eight columns in marble from the Caunes region symbolizing the eight magistrates support a pediment decorated with statues of Force and Justice. The north portico is crowned with statues of Clemence Isaure and Pallas, and the southern portico bears the images of Tragedy and Comedy. The imposing facade was replicated on the side facing the Square

de Gaulle in 1883-84.

After the Porte of Bachelier, a large stairway provides access to ceremonial rooms : the Salle Henri-Martin, the Salle du Conseil Municipal, the Galerie des Illustres. Paintings from the end of the 19th and the beginning of the 20th centuries glorify grand events in the city's history.

Henri Martin created an exceptional set of paintings ; some panels represent the Seasons, others show the banks of the Garonne (where Jean Jaurès can be seen in an off-white raincoat). The grand Galerie des Illustres, renovated at the end of the 19th century, has received paintings, busts and stucco works from the greatest of Toulouse's artists.

The Capitole is also the theater of the same name, which is located in the southern wing of the city hall. Once a great opera house, it is now too small to do justice to the sound of its orchestra and to meet the demand of a public which has traditionally adored such music.

THE RUE DU TAUR

The Rue du Taur leads from the Place du Capitole, which was laid out in the 18th and 19th centuries on the site of the large northern gate of the Roman city (the last remains of which were demolished in 1971), to the Saint-Sernin basilica. With its adjacent streets, where can be seen old schools and the municipal library (one of the largest in France), with its shops selling new and second-hand books, it continues the Bourg's University tradition dating from the Middle Ages. The presence of the Tour Maurand (a vestige of a 12th century fortified manor), of 17th and 18th century houses and the proximity of former convents provide an introduction to the city's complexity.

THE EGLISE DU TAUR

With its mighty façade topped by the cowled arches of the steeple, the Eglise du Taur fits into the alignment of the houses on the street, a disposition which has become relatively rare. Originally, the first chapel may have been built on the tomb of Saturnin (see Saint-Sernin). Around 1300, the church was rebuilt ; its single nave had three bays. During the next century, two larger bays were added onto the eastern section and amplified by lateral chapels and the choir. The whole was arranged in an original manner : between two chapels was built another, that for some time held the shroud of Cadouin (which has since been returned to the abbey). The shroud, which is said to come from Antioch, was transported to Toulouse during the Hundred Years War, and it is claimed that it worked a number of miracles. It was authenticated in 1935 as being of Moslem origin and dating from the early 12th century. The church's current dusty decor is somewhat sad. Nonetheless, on the south wall of the third bay of the nave, there remain traces of a 14th century painting showing thirty-eight persons representing the genealogy of Jacob.

Few Toulouse residents know of the Foix student hostel. Nonetheless, it is one of the rare 15th century buildings still standing in Toulouse, and it is a charming representation of the architecture of mediaeval University student hostels.

The portal and the steeple of the church of the Couvent des Cordeliers.

LE COLLEGE DE FOIX

Forgotten today in the charms of a secret garden, the College de Foix is the creation of a patron cardinal, Pierre de Foix, papal legate of Avignon. This religious foundation was to provide free housing for 25 poor and deserving students of civil law, canon law and theology. It was constructed by the head builder Jean Constantin between 1457 and 1460. The four galleries of the court provided access to various rooms, offices, dormitories, and bedrooms necessary for student life. To the West was built the chapel (demolished in the 19th century), whose keystone, engraved with the coat of arms of the cardinal, is preserved at the Musée des Augustins. The main buildings still dominates the college, with its angled turrets and its open windows in austere brick walls. A vast room on the ground floor held a precious library of manuscripts which were acquired by the cardinal after the death of the anti-pope Benoit XIII, sold to Colbert in the 17th century, and which are now stored in the Bibliotheque Nationale.

Two notable changes affected city life in the 13th century : the appearance of the mendicant orders and the creation of the University (1229). With the latter, a new type of structure was instituted ; the colleges, or student hostels. These were designed to house poor students and provide them with spiritual as well as material security. In 1243, a rich bourgeois, Vidal Gautier, founded the first one for 20 poor students. Until the beginning of the 14th century, the other hostels were created by the great monastic orders in order that monks (from Grandselve, from Moissac...) could study in Toulouse.

Then, in 1319 the Montlauzun hostel, and in 1337 the Verdale hostel introduced a more efficient formula : the hostel was to be a charitable foundation, for the eternal rest of the donor's soul, specifically oriented towards the University (the students had to know how to read and to show a capacity for learning) and with a spiritual goal (numerous religious rites were scheduled).

THE COUVENT DES CORDELIERS

The Cordeliers (a minor order of Franciscan friars) moved to Toulouse in 1222. Nothing remains of the early buildings and little of the large monastery built from the 13th to the 15th century. The church (13th to 14th century), of which remains the steeple, a piece of the wall of the apse and the portal, was built on a large scale: 86 meters long, 27 meters wide and 26 meters high. With a single nave, it had the same outer appearance as the church of the Jacobins : a pentagonal apse in prolongation of the nave, high buttresses linked by transverse arcs, chapels lodged between the buttresses. After being allotted in 1818 to the military, which used it as a fodder storehouse, it burned in 1871. Rather than restore it, the church was demolished. It was complemented by a large chapel on the southwest side ; built by Jean Tissandier, the bishop of Rieux, between 1322 and 1347, it was demolished in the first half of the 19th century. Statues of the apostles, of Franciscan saints, of Christ and the Virgin Mary, of Jean Tissandier as the donor as well as the recumbent statue from the bishop's tomb were taken from it and are preserved at the Musée des Augustins (except for two at the Musée Bonnat in Bayonne). The visitor can still admire the chapter house by entering the Forum des Cordeliers by way of the Rue des Lois.

THE CHAPELLE DES CARMELITES

Built beginning in 1622, the chapel is the only remaining vestige of the Carmelite convent, which reached almost to the site of the municipal library. Its architecture is simple, a single nave with four bays completed by a three-sided apse. Its vault is built of oak paneling with supporting ribs. At the end of the 17th century, J.-P. Rivalz decorated the high parts between the windows with paintings inspired by the Sistine Chapel. The decoration was completed in the middle of the following century by J.-B. Despax, who produced here what is considered as the masterpiece of the city's painting from that era. Three subjects of Carmelite meditation were illustrated : the incarnation of Christ with a part devoted to childhood, the wonders realized by the prophet Elijah and his disciple Elisha, the founders of the religious community on Mount Carmel and the glorification of Saint Theresa of Avila, the reformer of Carmel, canonized the year of the founding of the chapel.

The Musée Saint-Raymond, a former university student hostel built in 1523 by Louis Privat.

On the following pages :
The southern side of the Basilique Saint-Sernin. (Photo Jean-Paul Gisserot)

SAINT-SERNIN

The first bishop of Toulouse, Saturnin, was martyred in 250 A.D. ; while he was on the way to his church, he was recognized by pagans who blamed him for the failure of the sacrifices they offered to their gods. They tied him to a bull which tumbled down the steps of the Capitole temple, left the City by its northern gate and disappeared into the countryside. The body of Saturnin was buried by two women in the necropolis which laid on either side of the Route de Cahors. Hilaire, his successor in the fourth century, built a small wooden church above his tomb. Due to the large number of worshipers, and because the burial sites had multiplied around the holy grave, Bishop Exupere built a large basilica further North, to which the remains of the saint were transferred in 402 or 403. A monastery, mentioned in 844, was built to guard the tomb.

In the middle of the 11th century, this first church no longer met the needs of the many pilgrims who came to pray near the numerous relics stored in the sanctuary. In the third quarter of the 11th century, construction began on the chevet of the vast church which we know today, with its monumental transept, each wing of which includes two facing apses, and the choir surrounded by an ambulatory providing access to five radiating chapels.

Galleries are situated above the aisles of the transept and those of the choir bay ; their vaults buttress those of the upper portion of the chevet. At the intersection of the transept rises the steeple. At the very deepest part of this vast edifice, in the crypt, was kept the tomb of Saturnin (who became known as ''Sernin''), which the pilgrims could see through a small window. Outside, the terracing of the structure from the radiating chapels to the emergence of the steeple offers the eye a balanced progression, and the color contrast provided by the joint use of brick and stone gives life to this mighty structure.

Sculpture played a major role from the beginning of the basilica's construction, with close to 260 capitals on the inside and portals on the outside decorated with narrative scenes. The Porte des Comtes, constructed beginning in 1082-83, was monumentally decorated. Under the decorated cornices are three mutilated relief sculptures (the center relief depicted Saint Saturnin between two lions) which sit above the double passage. In the passage, the capitals evoke the parables of the wicked rich man and of Lazarus, representations of the

On the opposite page :
The chevet of the Basilique Saint-Sernin.

The interior of the Basilique Saint-Sernin.

The Porte des Comtes owes its name to the nearby burial ground which holds the tombs of the family of the counts of Toulouse in early Christian sarcophaguses, undoubtedly taken from the necropolis which surrounded the first basilica.

The inscription which runs along the upper part of the altar recalls that "the fraternity of the holy martyred Saturnin established this altar on which the divine rite shall be celebrated for the salvation of their souls and that of all God's faithful." It was signed by the sculptor Bernard Gilduin. The different sides of the table are adorned by relief sculptures; a bust of Christ carried by angels looking away appears on the forward side, on the left he is surrounded by the Virgin and the apostles ; other apostles are represented on the opposite side and the back is decorated with a frieze of birds facing one another.

theme of Salvation and Damnation.

In 1096, the work had progressed sufficiently to allow the installation of the table of the main altar. Pope Urban II himself consecrated the church and the alter.

In 1118, at the death of canon Raymond Gayrard, who headed the construction, the chevet was finished, the nave had reached the level of the high windows and was finished only in its three or four eastern bays. The nave continued the monumental portion of the transept, but with double aisles - a rarity during the Romanesque period. At the southern end, the Miègeville door received its decorations around 1115-1120. Carved figures support the upper cornice, the facade is decorated with the images of Saint Peter and Saint James the Greater. The tympan, the essential element of the portal, develops the theme of the Ascension. Slightly further back, the western portal should have surpassed it in splendor, but the two doors without tympan were surmounted with relief sculptures in marble which disappeared during the Revolution. Painted decorations covered the inside of the church beginning in the Romanesque period ; the recent removal of whitewash put on in the 19th century revealed fragments of the old paintings. The most complete composition is found in the northern portion of the transept : on the wall, the Resurrection of Christ takes up five panels, and the Glory of Jesus Christ is depicted on the vault. The construction of the church continued during the Gothic era : at the same time that the tomb of Saint Saturnin was being raised under a canopy and the crypts were built (they were enlarged in the 17th century), the construction of the nave also went on. The original plans were respected, as well as the concept of the vault, giving the church its interior unity. Work began again on the roofing of the entire building. The steeple was raised in the second half of the 18th century ; to ensure its stability, the supports of the transept crossing were reinforced. The Renaissance saw continuing work on Saint-Sernin ; new doors enlarged the entry to the crypts and new paintings covered the

Detail of Romanesque paintings in the northern portion of the transept, showing the Angel of the Resurrection and the Holy Women at the Tomb.

pillars of the transept, the walls and the vaults of the choir. 17th century builders wanted to provide more splendor for the presentation of the relics which were the wealth of the church. The relics, which had been kept in the ambulatory and its chapels, were placed in sculpted wood cabinets adorned with paintings and gilding, flanked with relief sculptures of great historical figures and surmounted by a pediment. This "Tour of Holy Bodies" has recently been returned to its place after having been removed by Viollet-le-Duc in the name of unity of style. With the work of the great architect and renovator, the 19th century was leave a strong imprint on the building. His alterations to the interior have been erased for the most part by a recent and welcome restoration carried out by the Chief Architect for

Historical Monuments Yves Boiret and Inspector Georges Costa. On the exterior, Viollet-le-Duc created recesses in the roof between the central nave and the tribunes, as well as at the level of the transept, so that the interior structure would be visible from the outside. He eliminated the tile coverings of the apses and replaced them with stone slabs. He also added ornaments, such as cornices supported by sculptures, diamond-shaped openings under the roofs of the major naves, arcature friezes under the roofs of the galleries, sculptures that have disappeared with time...

The condition of the upper portions of the building now requires fresh renovation, which must take into account the necessity of preserving the largest intact Romanesque church in

Europe.

The Eglise Saint-Sernin (promoted to the rank of a basilica in 1878) was, until the Revolution, closely linked to the abbey buildings which surrounded it. If nothing is known of the earliest installations, the Romanesque era left prestigious structures which were erased by the vandalism of the early 19th century. Among these were the great Romanesque cloister (several of its magnificent capitals are preserved at the Musée des Augustins), the chapter house, the abbot's dwelling and the canonical buildings. Today, in the middle of an oval square, the church emerges from an ocean of parked cars, slightly protected from their invasion by the fence of a small garden.

Musée Saint-Raymond, bust of the emperor Tiberius (14-37 A.D.).

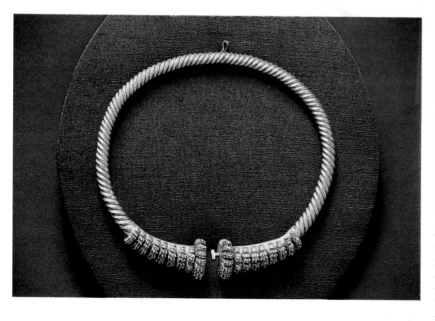

Musée Saint-Raymond, golden necklace from the second or third century B.C.

THE MUSEE SAINT-RAYMOND

The Musée Saint-Raymond is located in a former student hostel built by Louis Privat in 1523. Its collections cover a period stretching from the prehistorical era to the year 1000 A.D. In a picturesque garden which boasts a particularly beautiful view of Saint-Sernin, statues and menhirs stand alongside architectonic elements and funeral monuments, most of which come from the Roman city. The Bronze Age (the second millenium and the beginning of the first millenium B.C.) is represented by a large collection of hatchets, bracelets, fibulae and other items. The Iron Age collection is equally large, and its necklaces and bracelets made of gold from Fenouillet (near Toulouse) and Lasgraïsses (in the Tarn region) are known worldwide. The Mediterranean civilizations are well represented, and notably include Etruscan, Greek and Italian vases from the eighth to the first century B.C. A number of objects bring the Toulouse of the Roman era to life. A multitude of Roman trinkets (bronze figurines, mosaics, glass, ivory, a very large collection of keys and coins) also form part of the collection. But the strong point of the museum is undoubtedly the exceptional collection of antique sculptures, notably of imperial and private portraits (discovered mainly in the Villa de Chiragan, in Martres-Tolosane, and at Béziers). The statues and the mythological relief sculptures also include several masterpieces : copies of Myron's discobolus and Athena, Cnide's head of Venus, and a remarkable series of sculpted panels showing the labors of Hercules. An introduction to the Middle Ages is provided by sculptures, inscriptions and bronze liturgical vases. The museum, which is too small but is also very vibrant, continues to increase its collections through donations and objects retrieved from excavations. Since all of the works cannot be displayed due to a lack of room, temporary exhibitions are regularly organized to give visitors an idea of the richness of the reserves of one of France's most important archaeological museums.

SAINT-PIERRE-DES-CUISINES

The ancient Eglise Saint-Pierre-des-Cuisines is currently in poor condition and waiting for a new allocation and a renovation, and it only grudgingly reveals its historical and architectural interest. The story of the church began in the fourth and fifth centuries, with the establishment of a necropolis and then a funereal basilica outside of the walls of the antique City. In the 11th century, the church and its attached grounds were given by the count of Toulouse to the abbey of Moissac, which established a priory on the site. Saint-Pierre-des-Cuisines then experienced a period of architectural development whose scale has recently been revealed by archaeological excavations. A larger choir, better adapted to the needs of the monks, was built. It was destroyed at the end of the 18th century, but its remains can be seen to the east of the church ; a window and a triumphal arch (where the choir opened into the nave) constructed of the mixture of brick and stone which characterized the architecture of the end of the 11th century, as well as the eastern wall of the square steeple. The nave was later enlarged. To the west of the current church can be seen two parts. On the left between two buttresses is a wall which is thicker towards the bottom, penetrated by two arched windows (now walled up) and which belongs to the Romanesque nave. On the right, an elevation with one window, terminated by a mighty buttress, bears witness to the extension of the nave towards the South during the Gothic era.

On the southern side, the church displays its most monumental and romantic aspect. Buttresses separate bays illuminated by windows (their upper portion shows that the planned height was never achieved). A portal, employing Romanesque capitals from the years 1160-1180, was installed in this Gothic elevation. The capitals depict two narratives, one devoted to the life of Christ and the other to the life of Saint Peter. A rare mediaeval tomb, set inside a wall which once marked the border of the cemetery, shelters a sarcophagus. The arch in the middle of the recess is closed by

The portal and the mediaeval tomb of Saint-Pierre-des-Cuisines.

an arcature supported by four columns.

In the 16th century, the priory came under the control of the Carthusian order. At the time of the Revolution, the parish was transferred to Saint-Pierre-des-Chartreux and Saint-Pierre-des-Cuisines was transformed into a cannon foundry before becoming a warehouse within the arsenal of the Army of the Pyrenees.

SAINT-PIERRE-DES-CHARTREUX

The Carthusian monks of Saïx, near Castres, took refuge in the Bourg of Toulouse in 1569 after being chased from their monastery by Protestants. They began to build their monastery in 1602. The architecture of the church clearly demonstrated its basic function : a dome marked the site of the altar, towards the street the three-bayed nave received the faithful and at the other end a large chorus of six bays was reserved for the monks. For two centuries, the greatest artists of Toulouse succeeded one another in the church, creating one of the city's most beautiful collections of classical art.

The church was dedicated to the Virgin Mary and Saint Paul the Hermit in 1612. A first dome had just been finished, with a wooden ceiling, and Pierre Monge had sculpted the stalls of the monks. The decorations of the chorus grew richer, and in 1654 it was adorned with a series of paintings of scenes from the Gospel. In 1682, François Fayet painted a ten-panel work titled "Les Pères du Désert", alternating with panels showing the life of Saint Bruno.

The Eglise Saint-Pierre-des-Chartreux seen from the Northwest. Up until the Revolution, the church served as the principal monastery of the Carthusians. Today, it retains one of the most beautiful sets of classical art from the 17th and 18th centuries.

Before 1752, Pierre Lucas completed the set with relief sculptures representing the monastic, moral and theological virtues. In the 18th century, the first church was remodeled ; it was heightened (the old walled-in windows can be clearly seen) and the dome, surmounted by the statue of Saint John the Baptist was redone. François Cammas provided the artwork on the plastered vault of the dome, where the spirit of Antiquity manifested itself in the grand arches, the pilasters and the Corinthian capitals. He painted the monochrome designs on the arms of the transept and thought up the design of the altar. On the pedestal, François Lucas crowned the crucifix with two angels, also done in a very Roman spirit. The great delicacy of the angels' gestures, the disorder of the garments, the quality of the faces and the studied position of the bodies in order to avoid rigid symmetry all make these angels a group full of dynamism and grace, "surprising in the chapel of an order known for the rigor of its mortifications." (J. Rocacher)

But the riches of the church do not end there. There is also the wooden pulpit carved in the shape of the prow of a ship, the re-used Romanesque grilles and the sumptuous grilles of the 17th and 18th century. The organs were provided by the Jacobins ; the instrument was brought to the Carthusian church when it was dedicated to Saint Pierre and became the seat of the parish.

THE RAMPART OF THE BOURG

These considerable vestiges of the Bourg's mediaeval rampart have been conserved - or perhaps forgotten? - along a stretch 650 meters long. Four mighty towers still stretch along the straight rampart built in the 14th century and redone in the 16th century (nothing is known of the first rampart, dating from the 12th century). Numerous gates marked the points where city streets let out onto the neighboring countryside ; Porte du Bazacle, Las Crosses, Arnaud-Bernard, Pouzonville, Matabiau, Sardane, Villeneuve. Their memory remains in the names of nearby streets.

On the filled-in trenches and the wooden palisades of the City and the Bourg were established the boulevards which form the city's inner beltway.

THE GUE DU BAZACLE

The roadway of Bazacle recalls the old river ford which permitted the crossing of the river at any time. On the right bank were the mills of Bazacle as cited by Rabelais, owned by stockholders known as "bettors", from the end of the 12th century on. The architectural remains of this area may be visited during special events organized by the National Electric Company (EDF), which now owns the land. The visit is highly recommended, as it also allows access to a special site above the river which offers a superb view of the city.

THE SAINT-CYPRIEN DISTRICT

The waterfront facade of the Saint-Cyprien district is marked by two large buildings, the Hospice de la Grave and the Hôtel-Dieu Saint-Jacques, and by the large Prairie des Filtres. This neighborhood, frequently flooded despite the construction of dykes in the 18th century, owes its name to an ancient chapel dedicated to Saint Cyprian which once stood in the area. As the gateway to Gascony, it emerged as a center for customs and trade in the Middle Ages. The animation along the district's main artery - the Rue de la République leading to the Place Intérieure Saint-Cyprien - should not make the visitor forget the discreet charm of streets which still give it the atmosphere of a village.

THE HOSPICE DE LA GRAVE

Built at the water's edge at the end of the 12th century, the Hospice de la Grave housed the elderly, the incurably ill, abandoned children and "immoral" women. Its design, redone in the 17th century, was respected until the 20th century. Its independent buildings were each reserved for a category of residents, organized around interior courts equipped with wells, where the plants necessary for the feeding and care of the ill were

The buildings of the Carthusian monastery were requisitioned in the revolutionary era as an arsenal for the Army of the Pyrenees. Only a portion remains of the arcature of the main cloister, which was once neighbored by small houses which served as lodgings for the monks, permitting them to lead a life of solitude in the framework of their community. The site, nicely renovated and planted, is one of the most pleasant parks in the center of the city.

The rampart of the Bourg, from the 14th century (redone in the 16th century) is partially preserved along the Boulevard Armand-Duportal. From the Garonne, it reaches the Place Wilson. The boulevards were created along the emplacements of its trenches and its walls.

On the preceding pages :
The Chaussée du Bazacle and the Hospice de la Grave.

cultivated. Just before the Revolution, the hospice saw the addition of the neighboring buildings of the Couvent des Dames de la Porte, reaching to the Rue Réclusane and to the 16th century ramparts, two towers of which are still standing. The Chapelle de la Grave, whose construction began in 1750, saw its share of tribulations ; its wood foundations gradually needed to be replaced by others in concrete and its dome was restored several times, but its elegance breaks the austerity of the facades along the Garonne.

THE EGLISE SAINT-NICOLAS

The first chapel in the neighborhood, dedicated to Saint Cyprian, was one of the many buildings which disappeared without leaving a trace. The re-dedication in favor of Saint Nicholas placed this outlying district under the protection of the patron saint of sailors and drowning victims. The church was rebuilt in the 14th century, as shown by the keystones decorated with coats of arms, leaves and historical figures (including Saint Paul). The steeple was completed, with its upper levels ornamented by the traditional cowled arches, at the end of the 14th century (its spire was rebuilt in 1787).

Inside can be seen a reredos, perhaps the most beautiful in Toulouse, created according to the drawings of J.-B. Despax (1788), who also painted the paintings (with the death and apotheosis of Saint Nicholas in the center). Different-colored marbles, gilding and painting are associated in a single baroque theatrical movement intended more to affect worshipers' hearts than their minds.

The sculpted stonework of the portal, which is believed to date from the second half of the 15th century, is

On the opposite page :
The Eglise Saint-Nicolas, built in the 14th century, is the church of the outer neighborhoods of Toulouse. It offers a characteristic example of Gothic art in southern France, with its single nave, its chapels located between the buttresses and its large overhanging roof.

unfinished. The finesse and care used in the creation of the sculptures is impressive ; vegetable ornaments, small animals, etc. Six of the lateral niches received statues. Four of them, dating from the 15th century, reached the 20th century in decent condition but are currently in a poor state. The statues of Saint Cyprian and Saint Nicholas were created by the sculptor Rouzet (1863). In the tympan was a depiction of the adoration of the Magi, which has been replaced by a molded duplicate. The original has been placed in one of the chapels, where one can conveniently see it and appreciate the quality of the expressions, imprinted with a softness and pathos particular to the late Middle Ages.

THE HOTEL-DIEU SAINT-JACQUES

The Hôtel-Dieu Saint-Jacques presents a vast brick façade along the waterfront. It embraces the outlet of the last support of the covered bridge which linked the Port de la Daurade to the Saint-Cyprien district. This vast establishment is the heir of two hospitals, the Hôpital Sainte-Marie mentioned in the first third of the 12th century and the Hôpital Nord founded in 1235. Run by the fraternity of Saint-James beginning in the 13th century, it took its final form in the 16th century when some thirty charitable institutions were linked to it. At the outlet of the Pont-Neuf, three 17th century buildings open onto a French garden. To the East, a double flight of stairs marks the location of the former Rue aux Herbes which prolonged the covered bridge. To the right of the entrance is the tower where abandoned children were left. In the interior is located the Salle Saint-Jacques, where portraits of benefactors were often hung (the wooden ceiling dates from the 17th century), and the chapel. The building which closes off the garden contains the vast Saint-Lazare common room. The Hôtel-Dieu Saint-Jacques currently houses the local hospital administration, which is very interested in the building's renovation.

The Hôtel-Dieu Saint-Jacques, with its classical-era façade looking out over the Garonne.

THE WATER TOWER

The water tower was built in 1823. Its perfect design allowed the city to be supplied with water until 1860. After more than a century of abandonment, and thanks to the will and the obstinacy of the great photographer Jean Dieuzaide, it has been restored (the machinery is still visible) and transformed into a municipal photography gallery. The exhibitions change each month, drawing an ever-more numerous audience.

THE PONT-NEUF
AND THE WHARVES

The strength of the Pont-Neuf defies the centuries and the waters of the river which carried away so many constructions, such as the Pont de la Daurade (12th to 17th centuries). Like so many other ''Pont-Neuf'' in France, it is now

The city, the Pont-Neuf and the wharves seen from the Pont Saint-Michel.

one of the oldest bridges in the city. Its construction took more than half a century, beginning in 1544, and the greatest architects took part in the work.

The visitor standing on this bridge discovers the city from behind the wharves built under the impetus of Archbishop Loménie de Bienne at the end of the 18th century. The layout clearly shows the links which unite the city with the river, with the wharves, the ports, the mooring rings for the boats embedded in the strong brick walls. Old views of the city, seen in postcards and engravings, bring to life the incessant movement which reigned at the time ; today, it is a place for pleasant walks and, during warm weather, it becomes Toulouse's ''beach''. The great masses of the Eglise des Jacobins, of the Eglise de la Daurade and the Eglise de la Dalbade, their towers shooting above the crowded rooftops, invite us to continue our discoveries.

THE JACOBINS

The Dominican order was founded in Toulouse in 1215 by Saint Dominic and was recognized in 1217 by Pope Honorius III. The monks moved into a monastery on Rue Saint-Rome in 1216 and then acquired in 1229 - the same year that the university was created - the land where the church and its adjacent buildings would be constructed.

The church, designed with a rectangular layout and a strait chevet and covered only by a framework, began construction in 1229. It occupied the area which is taken up by the first five bays of the current nave. This church, lower than the current building, reflected the spirit of poverty of the first Dominicans. It was divided into two bays of unequal width, the northern one of which was used for sermons while the southern one was occupied by the monks' choir. The black marble tiles in the current floor show the foundation of the previous building, whose only vestige is the Romanesque portal situated on the western façade.

From 1244 to 1253, the lower part of the current chevet was added to the eastern portion of this sober building. The building was raised and vaulted between 1275 and 1292. It was separated into two equal parts by three tall cylindrical columns, while high windows provided abundant light. On February 2, 1292, Bertrand de Montaigu, the abbot of Moissac, celebrated the first mass on the altar of the chapel dedicated to the Virgin Mary. The contrast must have been great between the first church, low and unadorned, and this majestic chevet. The nave was later remodeled along the lines of the chevet, thanks to a donation of 4,000 gold pieces.

In 1368, a major event occurred ; the pope of Avignon Urban V expressed his wish that the body of Saint

On the opposite page :
The interior of the Jacobin church.

The Roman portal of the Jacobin church.
(Photo Jean-Paul Gisserot)

On the following pages : The famous
"palm tree" of the Jacobin church.

Thomas Aquinas (who died in Fosanova, Italy, in 1274) be buried in what he described as "the most beautiful and the most splendid" place, and he chose the Dominican church of Toulouse, with whose "grandeur and magnificence" he was familiar. On January 29, 1369, the body of the Saint was brought to the church with great pomp and ceremony. On October 22, 1385, the church was finally completed and was dedicated to Saint Thomas Aquinas. Its grandiose and original design made it a masterpiece of Gothic architecture in Southern France. It measures 80 meters long, 20 meters wide and its 22-meter-high columns are among the highest raised by Gothic architecture. One of the columns, slightly wider than the others, supports 22 ribs which radiate from it to the vault like the leaves of a palm tree.

In the 19th century, under military occupation, a one-meter-thick embankment placed the floor of the church at the same level as the ground outside. The church was divided vertically by the installation of two additional floors. Prosper Mérimée, visiting the site in 1840, denounced the vandalism which had disfigured the church.

With the arrival of the era of restorations, painted decor also reappeared. The walls were painted to resemble stone, the stones making up the ribs were painted alternately red and green, the coat of arms of Cardinal Godin was painted on the back side of the façade and friezes graced the entry to the chapels. The stained-glass windows of the chevet were reconstituted between 1923 and 1930 based on a simulation of the decor of the

The cloister and steeple of the Jacobin monastery.

opening on the wall corresponding to the steeple. The stained-glass windows in the nave were created in 1956 by Max Ingrand, who respected the chromatic design of the original windows conserved in the rose windows of the facade. Warm colors such as red and yellow dominated the southern end, while cooler tints such as blue and green were reserved for the northern nave.

The octagonal steeple rose alongside the church and was completed in 1298. Its four levels were decorated on each side by gemeled windows and topped by cowled arches. The steeple is crowned by an elegant arcature with small columns and capitals. It was originally topped by a 15-meter spire, constructed of a wood frame and covered with lead, which was destroyed during the Revolution.

The cloister was built from 1307 to 1310. The double marble columns support capitals whose motifs are generally plants. In the northeastern corner of the courtyard can be seen the remains of the wash basin. Only the western and the northern galleries (minus two arcades) survived in their authentic state ; the rest were redone between 1960 and 1970.

The chapter house, finished in 1301, owes its existence to the generosity of a priest, Arnaud Vilar, whose coat of arms is inscribed on several keystones. The room's ceiling is made up of six vaults on intersecting ribs. In the center, two slim prismatic marble columns carry the weight of the arches. A chapel formed by a vaulted seven-sided apse shelters an altar, painted in bright colors to resemble stone. In the 17th century, portraits of illustrious members of the order were painted in the room. The chapter, or assembly of the religious, was held in this room, which also received professors and their assistants from the mediaeval University.

The Chapelle Saint-Antonin, terminated in 1341, was built thanks to Dominique Grima, the bishop of Pamiers and formerly a friar at the monastery. Designed as a funeral chapel, it held the sepulchres of the religious and canons of the Cathédrale de Pamiers, and, in its center, that of its founder. The chapel is built in southern style as regards its proportions, but also as regards the large wall surfaces and vaults which invite rich decoration. In the vault and in the medallions can be seen the second vision of the Apocalypse (God the Father giving blessings, Jesus on his knees, busts of the 24 Old Men), and high on the walls, angels and musicians. Below are depicted forty episodes in the life of Saint Antonius, Saint Dominic and Saint Peter of Verona.

The refectory (1301-1303) is a vast room measuring 50 meters in length, with a wood ceiling and painting simulating the appearance of stone.

THE DAURADE

Named for the gold-based mosaics which ornamented it, the first Eglise Sainte-Marie la Daurade disappeared forever in 1761. Mystery continues to surround the origins, whether antique or early Christian, of this irregular polygon. Drawings, descriptions and vestiges of marble sculptures give an idea of its structure, of the splendor of its decor, and of the date of its origin, which is often cited as the fifth century. The interior was covered with precious mosaics. Higher up were scenes from the childhood of Christ, while towards the middle, the savior and the Virgin Mary were depicted surrounded by archangels, apostles and characters from the Old Testament who continue to appear lower on the wall. The cupola was pierced by a high rounded opening. The center of a monastery mentioned in 844, the church became the priory of Moissac in 1077. Renovation work was undertaken, and a nave was built, transforming the early Christian building into the choir of the new structure ; a Romanesque cloister spread out its galleries and its chapter house to the south of the church, accompanied by monastic buildings. In the 17th century, all of the buildings, in very poor condition, came under the ownership of the Maurists. The vaults of the nave had to be demolished in 1759. A new dome, placed over the choir in 1760, worsened the cracking of the old walls. The decision was taken to demolish both the church and the surrounding

This marble column, dating from the early Christian era and originally part of La Daurade, is located today in the court of a Toulouse Hôtel.

The Eglise de la Daurade and a 18th century house.

buildings ; the cloister was left intact until 1811. A first attempt at reconstruction, in 1765, was interrupted because the design did not fit in with the planned alignment of the docks. The current edifice began to rise in 1772. After a halt during the Revolution, during which the buildings were made into cotton and then tobacco manufacturing facilities, the church was finally dedicated in 1836. The colonnade and the pediment (1884), and the facade of the Palais des Arts completed the transformation of the old Benedictine monastery.

The interior of the church continues the solemn order of the Roman churches of the 17th century, with its great Corinthian pilasters, its overly low vaults and its transept with semicircular wings. The painter J. Roques from Toulouse created seven paintings for the choir. The southern wing of the transept houses, in an enameled terra-cotta receptacle, a widely venerated statue of the black Virgin dating from 1807. The statue was created after the memory of the 14th century original, which was burned during the Revolution, and represents the Marian piety which has existed in this spot perhaps as far back as the council of Ephesus in 431 A.D.

THE SHOPPING DISTRICT

The shopping district is concentrated between the rue Saint-Rome and the Rue des Changes on the one hand and the wharves on the other. It is characterized by the long shape of the blocks and the narrowness of the streets. Here are mixed together humble houses and mansions built after the fire of 1463 which have left the street facade to the stores and have reserved the inner courts for themselves. The very names of the streets recall the intense activity which took place here during the Middle Ages ; Rue des Changes (money changers), rue des Peyrolières (boilermakers), Rue de Tripière (butchers). We also must evoke the pastel plant, which was one of the major factors in Toulouse's growth during the second half of the 15th and the first half of the 16th

The façade of the Eglise de la Daurade, with colonnade and pediment. (Photo Jean-Paul Gisserot)

The Carrefour des Changes marks the intersection of the pedestrian Rue Saint-Rome and Rue des Changes, which retrace the route of the city's principal north-south artery in Antiquity, with Rue Peyras and Rue Temponnières. Here, we are in the very center of the mediaeval City.

centuries. This plant, after long and careful preparation, produced a dye which was the only one until the appearance of indigo to provide indelible blues. Several merchants scented the commercial potential of the process and found the necessary financing to put the product on the international market. The Assézat, Bernuy, Cheverry, Delfau and Boysson families demonstrated their financial success by the construction of prestigious homes in the very heart of the neighborhoods where they had developed their businesses. The arrival of Indigo from the Indies at a time when the pastel harvest was substandard, combined with the Protestant conflicts, put an end to this golden age.

PRIVATE MANSIONS

The first mansions, built around the end of the 15th century, are particularly notable for their modest dimensions. The mansion of P. Delfau (20, rue de la Bourse), built before 1500, is typical ; the street facade opens onto a boutique and a hallway leading to a first court. A second building, parallel to the first, looks out on a garden, the winding staircase is situated on a corner of the building, a small corbelled tower provides access to the attic and, from there, to a terrace. The large projects of the 16th century were accompanied by a complete set of ornaments for the entry court (the street facade often remained

austere). This is the case for the mansion that Jean de Bernuy had built in the first years of the 16th century. The oldest parts, the facade and the second court, still show Gothic design. Bernuy confided Louis Privat with the work on the first court, all in stone, which was finished in 1530. On the back side of the facade, two arches mark the ground floor and three mark the first floor. A large arch, perilously over-lowered, decorated with coffers, supports the first floor of the perpendicular wing lighted by two large lattice work windows. The exuberance of the decorations, which bears the mark of various designs that originated in northern Italy or the Loire region and then were reinterpret-

At the heart of the Musée de Vieux-Toulouse (rue du May) offers a collection of objects, paintings and souvenirs from the Toulouse of long ago. Owned by the Association des Toulousains de Toulouse, it is a must-see.

The stairway of Pierre Bruni's mansion (16th century), one of the few to have preserved its lighting niche.

On the left :
A detail of the Institut Catholique's fa-
çade facing the Garonnette. The Institute
is a former convent which was rebuilt in
the 17th century.

On the right :
The interior court of the Hôtel d'Astorg.

ed, displayed the power of Jean de Bernuy, es who was so rich that he guaranteed the ransom payment of François I. In return, the king visited his mansion in 1533.

But the Renaissance had entered a new phase in Toulouse ; the desire for classical composition emerged, architectural treatises circulated and were discussed in humanist circles. It is in this context that the Hôtel d'Assézat was born, with the contribution of the architect Nicolas Bachelier. Two groups of buildings are situated around a vast court and articulated around a majestic staircase. Their three levels, whose height decreases at each level, are each decorated with regularly-placed windows framed by columns whose capitals are, successively, Doric, Ionic and Corinthian. The window frames and the columns are in stone, and their light tones mixed with that of the brick create a dreamy atmosphere which adds to the exceptional harmony of the whole. On the back of the facade facing the street, a portico surmounted by a gallery raises its four rhythmic arches by columns bearing a frieze. The fourth side of the court was constituted by a common wall, which was enlivened by a corbelled gallery supported by lowered arches.

This Renaissance palace now houses the city's academic and intellectual Societies, the most ancient and prestigious of which is the Académie des Jeux Floraux, the heir to the Consistoire du Gai Savoir founded in 1323 by the "seven troubadours."

THE GARONNETTE

Before exploring the Rue de la Dalbade, the visitor should stand on the Pont de Tounis (1515-1516) which spanned the Garonnette, a natural arm of the Garonne which dried up in the middle of the century. On one side can be seen the picturesque clusters of houses and the beautiful outlet into the Garonne, while on the other side are the garden facades of old buildings. The Hôtel Le Masuyer and the Institut Catholique (formerly the Couvent de Sainte-Claire) form an architectural ensemble which is unique in the 17th century.

THE DALBADE

Seen from Saint-Cyprien, the church presents its facade topped by three small brick towers and, to the rear, its square steeple inspired by that of Sainte-Cécile d'Albi, is marked by a series of crenels at the level of the roof. This steeple, which since the 16th century had raised its quadrangular mass topped by a spire more than 80 meters above the ground (the highest in the city) collapsed in 1926, carrying the church vaults with it in its fall and destroying numerous works of art. Some of the thirty or forty busts

The Hôtel d'Assézat (16th century) is a veritable Renaissance palace. The north and east wings are articulated around a monumental stairway concluded by two terraces and surmounted by a skylight on an octagonal base.

Portal of the former Jesuit's college (18th century), currently the Lycée Fermat on rue Lakanal. (Photo Jean-Paul Gisserot)

sculpted in the 16th century by Bachelier and his students to adorn the steeple were saved from the ruins. Also saved were four splendid relief sculptures from the main reredos, which can now be viewed at the Musée des Augustins.

According to tradition, the Eglise de la Dalbade ("the white") replaced a chapel founded in the seventh century by an early saint. As a Marian sanctuary which was the property of the Daurade, it was rebuilt a first time at the end of the 11th century. But when a fire ravaged the neighborhood and the church in 1442, it was restored and most probably enlarged. It was the age when the district took on the general appearance which it has to-day, with the arrival of prosperous bourgeois and aristocrats. The work done on the church was undoubtedly insufficient, as an entire reconstruction was begun at the end of the 15th century. The five-sided choir was built from 1480 to 1490, followed by the steeple, the single nave flanked by chapels between the buttresses, and finally the portal. The portal demonstrates the spirit of the years 1530-1540 : if the concept remains Gothic (with the presence of a tympan - decorated in 1878 by Gaston Virebent - and a pier), the moldings, the decorative repertoire and the monumental framing of the doors, all undoubtedly belong to the Renaissance. The huge and flamboyant rose window, set in the brick wall, further increases the church's solemnity.

THE HOTEL DES CHEVALIERS DE SAINT-JEAN DE JERUSALEM

The Hôtel Saint-Jean was the grand priory of Malta until the Revolution. It raises its classical facade, composed of a central bay flanked by four identical bays, between the Eglise de la Dalbade and the Chapelle Saint-Jean. In the 17th century, the hospitallers had asked J.-P. Rivalz to replace the old Romanesque buildings, and he responded by designing a veritable Roman palace. These brilliant knights, with their aura of eastern prestige, took up residence here around the year 1115. Heirs to the holdings of the Tem-

Detail of the façade of the Eglise de la Dalbade (15th to 16th century); the Renaissance portal was completed in the 19th century with a tympan by the ceramist Gaston Virebent.

plars, they founded the grand priory of Toulouse in 1315. It is indispensable to enter the majestic porch with its brick vault, to see the court, which resembles a cloister, the vaulted chapter house and the grand stairway with its straight banisters. On the southern side, if the door of a small room is open, it is possible to see the last vestiges of the mediaeval church of Saint John. Two tombs are set in the wall, one Romanesque with an early Christian sarcophagus, the other Gothic, whose beautiful sarcophagus in sculpted stone is on display at the Musée des Augustins, in the old sacristy.

THE RUE DE LA DALBADE

Almost nothing in this street leaves the passerby indifferent. What the facades do not reveal must be searched for in the courts. Such is the case for the Hôtel de Bruni (a 16th century stairway tower), the Hôtel de la Mamye (a two-bayed facade with three floors of galleries, from the 16th century) and the Hôtel d'Aldéguier (a court from the early 17th century). In marked contrast is the Hôtel which dominates the passerby with its vain facade which gained it the name of the "Hôtel de pierre" ("mansion of stone"). Around 1535, Jean de Bagis bought several parcels of land and asked N. Bachelier to build his mansion, of which the northern and western wings remain. In the western wing, a magnificent portal, whose crown is carried by two statues, provides access to an Italian staircase. François de Clary remodeled the buildings in the 17th century and built the stone facade on the street with its colossal pilasters and relief sculptures. This last work was "completed" in 1857.

Facing page above:
Porch and court of the Hôtel Saint-Jean, formerly the grand priory of Malta during the 17th century (32, rue de la Dalbade).

Facing page below:
Detail and elevation facing the court of the Hôtel de la Mamye (31, rue de la Dalbade), from the 16th century. The three superimposed galleries correspond to the three classical orders (Doric, Ionic and Corinthian) found at the Hôtel d'Assézat.

Doorway to the stairway tower of the Hôtel du Vieux-Raisin (16th century), 36, rue du Languedoc.

Lodgings of the Hôtel Dahus (15th century) and the Tour de Tournoër (16th century). Other parts of the Hôtel Dahus are to be found in the Hôtel du Vieux-Raisin.

THE PARLIAMENT

The Languedoc Parliament met permanently in Toulouse beginning in 1443. The first of the provincial Parliaments, its organization was slowly improved. The Grand Chambre had two presidents (and a third beginning in 1460), and its work was prepared by the Chambre des Enquêtes. Beginning in the 16th century, the Chambre des Tournelles took responsibility for criminal affaires and the Chambre des Vacations (which functioned during vacation periods) and the Chambre des Requêtes were added on to the

On the preceding pages :
Interior court of the Hôtel de Pierre (25, rue de la Dalbade), opposite side of the street facade (17th century).

Parliament. In 1519, 30 councilors worked in the Parliament ; by the 17th century their number had increased to 150, accompanied by a crowd of magistrates, lawyers and clerks. Gradually, venality and nepotism exercised their effects.

The Parliament was seated in the Château Narbonnais, the former residence of the counts of Toulouse, which touched the southern gate of the ancient City on one side. The buildings were largely demolished in the 16th century. The architect J.-P. Laffon rebuilt the Cour d'Appel between 1828 and 1833 ; today it forms the Palais de Justice along with the Tribunal de Grande Instance (1854-52) and the Cour d'Assises (around 1840). Nonetheless, memories of the Parliament remain despite its dissolution in

1790, including the Salon Doré (15th century, 17th century decoration), the chapel and the Salon d'Hercule (17th century carved wood ceiling).

The members of Parliament saw their financial position increase at the same time as their appetite for splendor. Their urban dwellings are there to bear witness, as are they properties which they bought in the surrounding countryside. Their mansions fit the definition given by the architect d'Aviler at the end of the 17th century (quoted by P. Mesplé), that is "a distinctive house inhabited by a person of quality."

Facing page :
Portal of the court of the Hôtel de Pierre. Statue by N. Bachelier.

RUE DU LANGUEDOC AND RUE OZENNE

These two streets, laid out at the end of the 19th and beginning of the 20th centuries, destroyed the links which united the neighborhoods of Les Carmes and Saint-Etienne. Their recent creation must be taken into account in order to understand what remains of the Hôtel Bérenguier-Maynier (commonly called the Hôtel du Vieux-Raisin), the Hôtel Dahus, the Hôtel Baderon-Maussac and the Hôtel Potier-Laterrasse.

Rue Ozenne remains an impressive example of 15th century public architecture, as shown by the Hôtel Dahus, a tall building crowned by false machicolations from which emerge gargoyles. In the 16th century, the next owner undertook the construction of the hexagonal tower, which was completed by the parliamentary councilor Guillaume de Tounoër.

The Hôtel du Vieux-Raisin holds part of the lodgings which belonged to Pierre Dahus. Between 1515 and 1528, construction began on the central building, the beginning of the two wings and the two staircase towers, which were completed in the 16th century. Here, two periods of the Renaissance are expressed, with the first one appearing in the initial construction with the decoration of the doors and windows with pilasters decorated with candelabrum and surmounted by friezes of foliage. The second one is manifested in the portico and the framing of the windows created by the new owner Jean Burnet, where the caryatids recall the vigor of Nicolas Bachelier's work on the Hôtel de Pierre.

THE MUSEE PAUL-DUPUY

Installed in a 17th century mansion, the museum was built around the collections assembled by Paul Dupuy in the first half of the 20th century. Augmented by several donations and large purchases, it is one of the greatest French museums of decorative art. The clock collection (donated by Gélis) is exceptional. The arts of earthenware,

Facing page :
The Jesuit apothecary, from the Noviciat des Jésuites (which was located on Place de la Daurade), preserved at the Musée Paul-Dupuy.

Cloister and church of the former Augustinian monastery (14th century), which became the "Provisional Museum of the Midi of the République" in 1793, and is today the Musée des Augustins.

Musée des Augustins : Detail of Christ Descendu de la Croix, by Nicolas Tournier (1590-1639), one of the best examples of the Caravaggio school.

of glass, of ivory, of silver and gold, of clothing and the Salon de Musique evoke the art de vivre of past centuries. The 17th century Jesuit apothecary is perfectly at home here. The basement, with its brick vaults, serves as a framework for the presentation of invaluable works of art such as the "Cor de Roland" (11th century horn of ivory) or the 14th century altar facing decorated with medallions showing scenes from the Gospel and the life of Saint Francis. The museum also houses a large set of mediaeval and modern coins, and an extraordinarily rich collection of drawings and engravings which are periodically put on display.

THE MUSEE DES AUGUSTINS

Toulouse's municipal Musée des Beaux-Arts (painting and sculpture) is located in the former Augustinian monastery. Beginning here in 1793, the "Provisional Museum of the Midi of the République" assembled collections coming from the Capitole and the Parliament, from churches and monasteries, from emigrant hostels and learned societies, along with all other antiquities "capable of serving in the future for the history of the commune." The cloister (finished in 1396) provides access to sacristy (14th century), the Chapelle Notre-Dame de Pitié (1341) and to the chapter house (14th to 15th centuries), all of which offer an architecture of great quality. The surroundings are perfectly suitable for the presentation of Gothic sculptures ; funereal works (a remarkable recumbent statue from the tomb of Guillaume Durant), an exceptional set of statues from the Chapelle de Rieux, a representation universally known as "Notre-Dame de Grasse" (from the Jacobins church). The famous set of Romanesque sculptures is displayed in the western part of the cloister, in a late 19th century building which replaced the 14th century refectory, which was destroyed in order to admit the construction of the Rue d'Alsace-Lorraine. Wreckage from the vandalism which ravaged Toulouse in the 19th century, the capitals of the cloisters of Saint-Sernin, La Daurade and Saint-Etienne and their great relief sculptures evoke all of the lost 12th

Musée des Augustins, a set of statues from the Chapelle de Rieux (14th century) ; in front, the bishop Jean Tissandier offers his chapel to God.

century monuments, the iconographic inventions and the stylistic mutations which they held. Also in the collection are many other equally remarkable Romanesque works from Narbonne, Saint-Gaudens, Lombez and Saint-Rustice. A very important series of engraved mediaeval inscriptions (from the 11th to the 16th centuries) can be seen in an adjacent gallery. The church (14th to 15th centuries) was devoted to religious art (Cardinal Godin's Christ, from the 14th century, Rubens' Crucifixion). The painting section is no less rich, with early Flemish and Dutch painters and works from the 17th to 19th centuries, notably by artists from Toulouse such as Tournier, Chalette, A. Rivalz, Roques, etc. The Salon Rouge houses, in a well-adapted presentation, works by 19th century painters such as Corot, Ingres, Delacroix, Constant and Laurens.

THE SAINT-ETIENNE DISTRICT

Beyond the Rue d'Alsace-Lorraine and the Rue Ozenne, in the direction of Saint-Etienne, stretches a rich neighborhood of 16th, 17th and 18th century houses and mansions. The Rue Croix-Baragnon includes a series of homes of surprising quality. The "maison romane" ("Romanesque House") (early 14th century) has preserved, despite repeated renovations, a set of five gemeled windows, linked by a frieze showing animals flanking ceremonial shields. Further on, the classical Hôtel de Castellane (18th century) faces the street with its monumental portal surmounted by terra-cotta lions. The facade of the Hôtel de Bonnefoy (renovated in 1729-1730) still bears the trace of medieval gemeled windows, and in its court rises a beautiful Gothic tower (1513). A number of balconies are made of forged iron and date from the 18th century ; Bernard Ortet realized the balconies at the Hôtel Bonfontan (N° 41). The neigh-

On the opposite page :
In the court of the Hôtel d'Ulmo (rue Ninau), a stairway topped by a very elegant canopy provides access to a stairway with straight banisters (16th century).

Detail of the façade of the "Romanesque House" (14th century) ; the set of gemeled windows represents a medieval design of which few rare examples are still conserved in Toulouse.

18th century terra-cotta lions surmounting the portal of the Hôtel de Castellane on Rue Croix-Baragnon.

Stalls in the cathedral, sculpted by Pierre Monge after the great fire which ravaged the choir during the night of December 9th, 1609.

On the facing page :
An interior view of the Saint-Etienne cathedral ; the nave (11th-13th centuries) and the choir (end of the 13th century) are not on the same axis. The choir bears witness to a gigantic 13th century plan to rebuild the cathedral, which called for the elimination of all previous existing edifices. Only the choir was carried out, and the old nave was attached to the new construction for better or for worse.

boring streets are equally rich in such sights. For example, the Rue Ninau includes the Hôtel d'Ulmo. On the street, a high wall penetrated by a large carriage entrance and surmounted by a passageway links the two wings of the great brick building. The main building opens out onto the court by way of a stairway surmounted by a canopy with beautifully shaped columns and Ionic capitals which itself provides access to a stairway with straight banisters, one of the first of its kind built in Toulouse (along with that of the Maison de Pierre).

THE CATHEDRALE ST-ETIENNE

From the outset, the cathedral dis-

concerts many people due to its strange form, the result of architectural modifications carried out since the Roman era. In the early Christian era, the episcopal group established itself on the antique rampart near one of the gates. The buildings which occupied the site in the early Christian era remain unknown. We know that the Bishop Isarn found, upon his arrival at the episcopal seat (1071) a ruined and deserted church. In the general current of the Gregorian reforms, he improved the life of the canons who looked after the cathedral and undertook to rebuild the edifice. The vestiges can be seen on the walls of the current nave (particularly in a bulls-eye window where stones and

bricks alternate, visible from the garden). The church was transformed at the beginning of the 13th century ; the outer walls of the Romanesque edifice were used to support the vast nave which we now know. The cathedral affirmed some of the developing principals of Gothic architecture in the Midi : a vast space without side aisles, originally intended to be ribbed but eventually covered by a single vault 19.5 meters wide between 1220 and 1240. The vaults, which were very rounded, were supported by rectangular ribs, lateral arches and other supporting structures that were grounded on pilasters by the intermediary of the Romanesque capitals, which were thus put to new use.

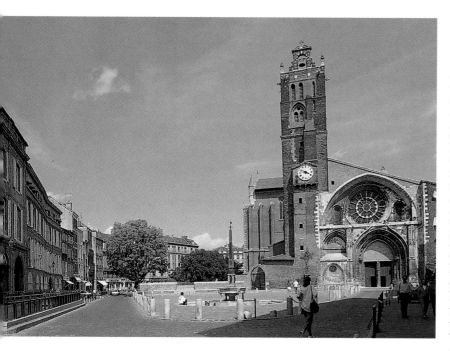

Place Saint-Etienne, whose "griffoul" is the city's oldest fountain (16th century). 17th and 18th century houses border this triangular square, which is completed by the facade of Saint-Etienne.

Stained-glass window in the cathedral.

To the West, the facade received a large rose window (most of whose elements were handed over to the Musée des Augustins following the most recent restoration). On the inside, the window overlooked a gallery covered with cowled arches. Only the three western bays of the building have been preserved, we know nothing of the placement of the chevet. Another church existed further to the East, but it completely disappeared during the construction of the current choir. The choir was the result of the immense project envisioned by the grand prelate Bertrand de L'Isle-Jourdain ; to level all previous buildings and undertake the construction of a completely new cathedral in a style close to that of the cathedral of Narbonne, which belonged to northern French architecture. Towards 1272, the choir began to be built, and in huge proportions. Twice as large as the nave, including five bays, surrounded by an ambulatory and radiating chapels. The death of the bishop, and the resulting loss of financing, the dismemberment of the diocese in 1317 and then the general crisis of the 14th century, all contributed to the halt in construction. The work was covered with a "temporary" wooden roof. After several attempts restart construction under Archbishop Bernard du Rosier, Jean d'Orléans (1503-1533) built a large pillar which marked the beginning of a transept, but which was never completed. In 1609, a fire destroyed the wooden roof and the church's furnishings. In order to avoid the repetition of such a disaster, the archibishop and the canons decided to vault the choir, and the architect Pierre Levesville was given the job. He raised the height of the windows and closed the vault at 28 meters above the ground instead of the 40 initially planned. The choir served for the canons and the archbishop (the worshipers were placed in the nave, which was more or less well connected to the choir). Pierre Monge sculpted the choir stalls. It was only at the beginning of the 20th century that the link between the two parts was completed by the creation of the northern portal. The western portal had been splendidly rebuilt in the 15th century by the archbishop Pierre du Moulin.

The steeple shows the same stratification ; on a Romanesque portion which was extended in the Gothic era, Jean d'Orléans built the current steeple.

It is thus this surprising juxtaposition of amputated and incomplete edifices which forms the cathedral today. But far from being isolated, it is the center of a very active neighborhood which has seen its most prestigious landmarks disappear one after another. The district was formerly marked to the East by the City rampart, to the North by the cathedral, to the West by the seat of the diocese (the building, reconstructed in the 18th century has been taken over by the prefecture) and to the South by the canons' lodgings. A large cloister was attached to the southern end of the cathedral, and its arcature was formed of columns which were alternately simple and gemeled ; the angles of the galleries were formed of pillars decorated with marble relief sculptures. In the eastern gallery was the chapter house, which was the source of the elegant and refined relief sculptures representing the apostles, created by Gilabertus and his workteam during the years 1135-1140 (now housed in the Musée des Augustins).

The cloister was delimited to the south by the Eglise Saint-Jacques, whose origins undoubtedly go back to the early Christian era. This very large group of buildings disappeared in 1811 following the decision to extend the Rue Sainte-Anne - which had previously ended at the cloisters - to the Porte Saint-Etienne. The Chapelle Sainte-Anne was built around 1830 in the place of the Eglise Saint-Jacques, in a neo-Roman style and along a north-south axis.

THE GRAND-ROND AND THE PROMENADES

From the Cathédrale Saint-Etienne, the Allées François-Verdier lead to the Grand-Rond. In the second half of the 18th century, Toulouse was receptive to new ideas regarding urban development, whose goal was to increase the well-being of the inhabitants while simultaneously improving the city's economic potential. It is in this perspective that we must regard projects

A 18th century transom at 9, Place du Parlement.

The Eglise Saint-Jérôme, built between 1622 and 1625 by the architect Pierre Levesville (who also built the vaults of the Cathédrale Saint-Etienne after the fire of 1609).

Detail of a 19th century house on Place de la Trinité ; the 19th century taste for ornamentation and classicism is manifested here by a Roman design complemented by statues of Mercury and Plenty.

In the Jardin des Plantes, which is frequented year-round by thousands of children, a number of vestiges of old buildings which were facing demolition have been installed. This picture shows a section of the city's ancient rampart which served as the foundation of a medieval home.

The Musée Georges-Labit : the pediment of Preah Pithu, in sandstone, from the end of the 12th or the beginning of the 13th century. Georges Labit assembled an essentially ethnographic collection which included arms and objects from everyday life. Today, the museum houses a variety of objects from Southeast Asia which is the largest in France outside of Paris. The museum also possesses Egyptian antiquities.

such as the construction of the wharves, the Canal de Brienne, Place du Capitol and Place Saint-Cyprien, and of the Grand-Rond. In the latter case, the prime developer was Louis de Mondran. From the Grand-Rond, a vast oval garden with an ornamental pond, radiated six large avenues. In each of them, the center divider was planted and two lanes were reserved for traffic. The project was carried out between 1752 and 1754, but the housing construction program which was to have accompanied was never put into effect.

THE JARDIN DES PLANTES AND THE MUSEUM D'HISTOIRE NATURELLE

The barefoot Carmelites had established their monastery outside the city walls, near the Porte Montgaillard. The first mass was celebrated in the monastery's unfinished church in 1623. Initially dedicated to Saint Joseph, it became the parish of Saint Exupère in 1807 and its classical cloister was preserved. During the Revolution, the naturalist and future mayor of Toulouse Philippe Picot de Lapeyrousse moved the plants of the Jardin de la Sénéchaussée close to the former monastery ; thus was born the Jardin des Plantes. In 1806, on the grounds of the former monastery, he created an establishment destined for the study of the natural Sciences, which three years later became the Faculté des Sciences. The Muséum d'Histoire Naturelle officially opened its doors in 1865.

The museum's treasures are great and varied. At the beginning, they were made up of the large collections assembled by botanists such as Picot and Laperouse and pre-historians such as E. Cartailhac or the Abbot Breuil. The latter two created the first gallery in the world devoted to the newly-invented science of pre-history, of which they were the pioneers. Mammals, both skeletons and living creatures, and birds, belonging to European and exotic species were presented in the beautiful rooms built in the 19th century. Anthropology and ethnology were also represented. The strong point of the museum is undoubtedly is paleontological collections, which are known throughout Europe.

Exterior view of the Musée Georges-Labit ; this neo-Moorish style villa was built by Georges Labit to house the collections which he brought home from his eastern voyages.

The Canal de Brienne was dug in the 18th century to link the Garonne upstream from Bazacle with the Midi Canal. The two canals met at the Bassin de L'Embouchure and the meeting point is market by the Ponts-Jumeaux, decorated with a large relief sculpture created by François Lucas (1775).

MUSEE GEORGES-LABIT

Toulouse owes its surprising museum of Oriental art to Georges Labit, a son born to merchants from Toulouse in 1862. Attracted by distant voyages from a young age, he discovered Asia and brought back photographs and objects including stamps, weapons, porcelain and ivory from Japan. After his death, his father donated the collections which he had as-sembled and the curious neo-Moorish style villa which he had built to the City.

Since then, the collection has been enriched with an exceptional set of Khmer and Cham sculptures, from India, China, Tibet and elsewhere. The Musée Georges-Labit, which also includes some very beautiful Egyptian antiquities, is also the only French museum outside of Paris to offer such a wide panorama of objects to visitors in such a superb building.

The Garonne, the Hospice de la Grave and the Chaussée du Bazacle. Toulouse remains inseparable from its river, which allowed it to develop throughout its history. (Photo Jean-Paul Gisserot)

LEGENDES DU PLAN

1. Manufacture des Tabacs (XIXᵉ s.)
2. Moulins et usine du Bazacle.
3. Vestiges du grand cloître des Chartreux (XVIIᵉ s.)
4. Ancien séminaire Calvet (XVIIIᵉ s.)
5. Ancien hôtel Dubarry.
6. Ancien séminaire Saint-Charles (XVIIIᵉ s)
7. Ancien collège de Périgord (XVIIᵉ s) et tour Maurand (XIIᵉ s.)
8. Chapelle des Carmélites (XVIIᵉ s)
9. Ancien Magasin «Au Capitole» (début XXᵉ s.)
10. Eglise Sainte-Marie-des-Anges (XIXᵉ s.)
11. Façade de l'immeuble «La Dépêche» (XXᵉ s.)
12. Hôtel du Sénéchal.
13. Ancien collège de l'Esquile (XVIᵉ-XVIIᵉ s.)
14. Vestiges du couvent des Cordeliers (XIIIᵉ - XIVᵉ s.)
15. Collège de Foix (XVᵉ s.)
16. Ancien couvent des Dames du Sac (XVIIᵉ s.), puis hôpital Larrey.
17. Ancienne caserne de la Mission (XVIIᵉ s.)
18. Hôtel de Bernuy.
19. Hôtel de Maleprade.
20. Café «Le Bident».
21. Hôtel Duranti.
22. Eglise Saint-Jérôme (XVIIᵉ s.)
23. Ancienne commanderie Saint-Antoine du T. (XVIIᵉ s.)
24. Hôtel de La Fage.
25. Hôtel de Guillaume Bernuy.
26. Hôtel de Sapte.
27. Tour de Pierre Séguy (XVᵉ s.) et hôtel du capitoul Jean Bolé.
28. Hôtel Dumay et Musée du Vieux-Toulouse.
29. Hôtel Comère.
30. Ancien cloître du couvent des Ursulines et ancienne Poste.
30 bis. Tour de Jean de Gayssion.
31. Hôtel Lagorrée.
32. Tour des Ysalguier (XVᵉ s.), ancien hôtel d'Espagne.
33. Hôtel d'Olmières.
34. Hôtel de Nupces.
35. Hôtel de Pierre Delfau.
36. Hôtel d'Assézat.
37. Hôtel du capitoul Ricardy.
38. Tour Vinhas (XIIIᵉ s.)
39. Logis de Boysson et hôtel de Cheverry.
40. Maison d'Arnaud de Brucelles.
41. Maison du capitoul Jean de Boscredon.
42. Hôtel Delpech, (tour XVIᵉ s.)
43. Hôtel d'Astorg et Saint-Germain.
44. Hôtel Desplats.
45. Tour de Serta (XVIᵉ s.)
46. Hôtel Dassier.
47. Hôtel de Tornié de Vaillac.
48. Maison du XIXᵉ s.
49. Ancien collège Saint-Martial (XIVᵉ - XVIᵉ s.)
50. Hôtel Dupin.
51. Maison Calas.
52. Maison du XVIIᵉ s.
53. Hôtel de Pierre Bruni.
54. Hôtel de la Mamie.
55. Hôtel d'Aldéguier.

56. Hôtel de pierre.
57. Hôtel Saint-Jean.
58. Hôtel Molinier ou de Felzins.
59. Hôtel du baron de Montbel.
60. Hôtel de Villepigne.
61. Hôtel Le Mazuyer.
62. Hôtel de Chalvet, puis de Pins.
63. Maison de saint Dominique et ancien couvent des Réparatrices.
64. Hôtel du capitoul Jérôme Taverne et tour de Noël Rolle.
65. Hôtel de Guillaume de Lespinasse.
66. Hôtel du capitoul Jean Marvejol.
67. Hôtel d'Olivier Pastoureau (tour XVIᵉ s.)
68. Hôtel Reversac de Celès de Marsac.
69. Hôtel Boissy.
70. Chapelle et cloître du prieuré Saint-Antoine-du-Salin.
71. Temple, ancienne Trésorerie royale.
72. Tour du capitoul Pierre de Ruppe.
73. Hôtel de Paucy, dit «Maison de la Belle Paule».
74. Hôtel Fajole.
75. Eglise du Jésus (XIXᵉ s.)
76. Chapelle de Nazareth (XVIᵉ s.)
77. Hôtel Davisard.
78. Hôtel de Potier-Laterrasse (façade sur cour Renaissance).
79. Tour de Guillaume Carreri.
80. Hôtel Labat de Mourlens.
81. Hôtel du Vieux-Raisin.
82. Galerie de l'hôtel de Pins.
83. Hôtel de Ciron.
83 bis. Maison de Pons Imbert.
84. Hôtel de Castellane.
85. «Maison romane»
86. Hôtel et tour de Bonnefoy.
87. Hôtel de Ramondy.
88. Hôtel de Candie de Saint-Simon.
89. Hôtel de Puivert.
90. Hôtel de Campistron.
91. Hôtel d'Orbessan.
92. Tour de Raynier et hôtel de Virvin.
93. Hôtel d'Espie.
94. Hôtel d'Ayguevives.
95. Hôtel du capitoul Pierre Dahus et tour des Tournoër.
96. Hôtel Mansencal.
97. Hôtel de Pennautier.
98. Hôtel de Tappie de Vinsac.
99. Hôtel du XVIᵉ s.
99 bis. Hôtel de Sacère-Murat.
100. Hôtel de Castelpers.
101. Hôtel de Sevin-Mansencal.
102. Hôtel de Panat.
103. Hôtel Bonfontan.
104. Hôtel de Froidour.
105. Hôtel du capitoul Jean Catel.
106. Hôtel du conseiller de Maran.
107. Hôtel de Cambon.
108. Hôtel du Bourg.
109. Ancien bâtiment des Archives du diocèse (XVIIIᵉ s.)
110. Hôtel Lestang (XVIIᵉ s.)
111. Maison du XVIIᵉ s.
112. Hôtel du comte de Paulo.
113. Hôtel d'Ulmo.
114. Hôtel de Castagné d'Auriac.
115. Palais Niel.
116. Hôtel Thomas (vestiges de l'hôtel de Pins)
117. Hôtel Dupuy-Montaut.
118. Monastère des Feuillants.

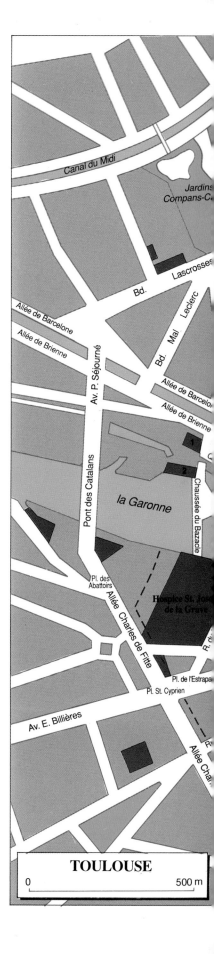

TOULOUSE

0   500 m

Front cover : The cloister and belltower of the Augustins church.
Back cover : The famous ''palm tree'' of the Jacobins church.

© Copyright 1992 - Editions SUD-OUEST. Ce livre a été imprimé et broché par Pollina à Luçon - 85 - France. La photocomposition a été réalisée par ALFA-CSR à Bordeaux - 33. Mise en page du studio des Editions Sud-Ouest à Bordeaux. Photogravure couleur de Bretagne Photogravure à Bruz - 35. La couverture a été tirée par l'imprimerie Raynard à La Guerche de Bretagne - 35, et pelliculée par Pollina - 85.
ISBN : 2.87901.035.7 - Editeur : 228.02.04.02.94 - N° d'impression : 64915 - B.